"Mike Martin is a motivator, encourager, and teacher to athletic TEAMS, business TEAMS, and people in general. He has given a solid footprint for developing TEAM unity, capitalizing on the success it brings TEAMS, and also how to protect the unity you establish. Mike challenges the TEAM member and the TEAM leader in his book Turning Silver Into Gold. It is a must read book that will benefit anyone who reads it."

-**Nick Mingione**
Head Men's Baseball Coach
University of Kentucky

"Mike Martin is the glue that held our team together. He showed us how to lead by example, how to love each other better, and how to keep God first through all of life's highs and lows. On our historic run to the Summit League Championship, Mike was our leader. His impact lasts a lifetime, long after the clock hits zero of that final game. Reading 'Turning Silver Into Gold' and applying its principles will help you and your team achieve more than you ever thought you were capable of."

-**Kyler Erickson**
University of Nebraska, Omaha Men's Basketball
2016 Allstate NABC Good Works Team
National Speaker and Color Analyst for ESPN+

"Turning Silver Into Gold is an easy read with great principles and ideals that encourage success in sports, business, and school. I am grateful for the opportunity to have read it and to be able to apply it to my business."

-**Jim Abraham**
Owner, Abraham Heating and Air Conditioning, Inc.

"Team unity is a huge part of any great teams success. I look back how close our 2013 College World Series team was and that played a huge role in our success. We believed in one another and came together like no team I have ever been a part of. One bad seed can poison a whole field and that could be the difference between a losing season and championship team! Turning Silver Into Gold is a book that will help teams Understand, Achieve and Protect Team Unity and excel together to a Championship Level!

-Hunter Renfroe
San Diego Padres
Outfielder

"As a freshman in college I quickly gravitated to Mike Martin he was a man of faith and character. He motivated me through the word and past experiences. I appreciate everything he has done for me. To this day he still works with me, helping me be a leader of our team on and off the field. Mike also sends me encouraging words that are always right on time and inspire me. Our relationship will always be strong and will stand the test of time and distance."

-Shaquil Barrett
Tampa Bay Buccaneers
Linebacker

In a world filled with its share of divisiveness and discord, this engaging "power read" by Mike Martin reminds readers that unity is an absolute essential in both BEING a team player, and in LEADING a team to victory and *sustainable* success.

Martin astutely provides practical concepts and strategies for developing high performing teams rooted in unity while sharing a multitude of relevant examples from teams, coaches, players, organizations and groups that have effectively mastered these principles.

Whether you're leading in athletics, business, ministry, the nonprofit sector, education, or another sphere of influence, applying the golden nuggets Martin shares in *"Team Unity"* will bless you in further anchoring yourself and your team in the most fundamental principle of unity."

-**Amie Gambonian**
Executive Leadership Coach
WHO YOU ARE
Leadership Coaching and Consulting

"All successful teams are made up of members who put others before themselves. Mike Martin embodies this simple principle, demonstrating a heart for others and a willingness to serve that comes through in his daily interactions and encouragements. Mike is a servant leader in the truest sense."

-**Scott Stricklin**
Director of Athletics
University of Florida

TURNING SILVER INTO GOLD

TURNING SILVER INTO GOLD

UNDERSTANDING, ACHIEVING AND PROTECTING TEAM UNITY

Michael H. Martin

© 2018 by Michael H. Martin

All right reserved. No portion of this book may be reproduced, stored in a retrieval system, or transmitted in any form or by any means – electronic, mechanical, photocopy, recording, scanning or other- except for brief quotations in critical reviews or articles without the prior written permission of the author.

Printed in the United States of America

CONTENTS

Acknowledgements   xii

Foreword   xiv

Introduction   xix

Part 1   UNDERSTANDING TEAM UNITY

1. TEAM UNITY DEFINED   28

Part 2   THE MEANS TO ACHIEVING TEAM UNITY

2. HAVING ONE VISION   42
3. SACRIFICE   57
4. COMMITMENT   73
5. SELF-LESS-NESS   81
6. CHARACTER AND INTEGRITY   102

CONTENTS

Part 3 THE COACHES ROLE IN ACHIEVING TEAM UNITY

    7. SETTING THE EXPECTATION EARLY ON   118
    8. BE A LEADER WORTH FOLLOWING   133

Part 4 THE RESULT OF TEAM UNITY

    9. THE ABSENCE OF FEAR   145

Part 5 PROTECTING TEAM UNITY

    10. ELIMINATING THE THREATS   155
    11. ENJOY THE JOURNEY – TOGETHER   165

ACKNOWLEDGEMENTS

Thank you to my wife, Debby, for supporting me and my passion for leadership, unity and athletics. I fall short more than I succeed but would not be the man I am today without the woman in you that is behind me. Thank you- I love you.

Thank you to our wonderful children, Caleb, Anna, Chloe', Lily, Clara and Seth for being road warriors and going with me when I go speak. Thank you for always thinking the best of me and believing in me. I cannot imagine life without each of you in it. You make your mother's and my life complete.

Foreword

Mike Martin has played an important role in the evolution of the University of Nebraska Omaha athletics department since 2009. I had the good fortune and pleasure to meet Mike early in my appointment as Athletic Director in the spring of 2009. Mike communicated his interest in meeting regularly with me for personal enrichment and spiritual growth. I found our meetings to be extremely valuable and profitable! Mike expanded his passion for others by extending his time beyond my office and became available to the entire staff and student population. Mike has worked extensively with several of our student-athletes and coaches-his impact has been real and tangible.

Foreword

Mike Martin has taken on a difficult, but important topic-Unity. Turning Silver Into Gold seeks to help solve why some organizations, churches, teams etc. accomplish great excellence while others make little impact. Mike has personally been mentored by great men of faith that helped mold his worldview on what unity is and how best to ensure its impact. Mike has watched the power of unity on display-the achievement that comes despite discrepancies in talent. Similarly, Mike has watched disunity destroy culture fundamentally critical for organizational success.

Mike models much of what is presented in Turning Silver Into Gold; A selfless attitude, servant leadership, sacrifice, and a commitment to character.

Foreword

I particularly enjoyed the "principle of priority" and the relationship between commitment and sacrifice. Unity of purpose demands a commitment to integrity and character- you may well ask yourself the same question Mike poses "The question is will we compromise our integrity when faced with a temptation or will we hold true to the commitment of the goal and the team?"

I have learned a lot about leadership and unity of purpose from Mike. Modeling positive leadership and "sowing seeds of leadership that might reproduce" are, in fact, the responsibility of all leaders. Certainly those "seeds" don't die as long as they are placed in the correct environment. I hope you are refreshed, encouraged, and challenged by reading this book.

Foreword

Great organizations need to foster an environment of unity for any hope of reaching their true potential. Establishing leaders who understand what unity is, how it is fostered and ultimately maintained will be a critical starting point.

-Trev Alberts

Athletic Director and Vice Chancellor
University of Nebraska, Omaha
- 2015 Inductee to the College Football Hall of Fame
- 5th overall pick of the 1994 NFL Draft
- Former Linebacker Indianapolis Colts
- 1993 Football Consensus All-American, Nebraska Cornhuskers
- 1993 Dick Butkus Award Winner
- 1993 Jack Lamb Trophy Award Winner

Introduction

Real, genuine Team Unity is the key to any team's success. Team Unity is crucial to the team having a chance to be successful. It is vital to gather and deploy the resources that will enable you and your team to achieve team unity as expeditiously as possible. This book will provide athletes, coaches, owners, CEO's and other high level leaders useful information on what Team Unity is, how it is achieved and then protected.

Over the years there have been many successful athletic teams; success for the purposes of this book is considered as a team achieving its mission and common goal. Consider teams like the UCLA Bruins Basketball under Coach Wooden; 10 National Championships. The 1957 – 1969 Boston Celtics (11 Championships in 13 years), North Carolina's Women's Soccer (nine straight National Championships from 1986 – 1994) and the

Introduction

Edmonton Oilers (Five NHL Stanley Cup Victories from 1984 – 1990).

There have also been some very unsuccessful teams over the years: the 1960 Dallas Cowboys (0 – 11), 2005 – 2006 Oakland Raiders (6 – 26), the 1939 Saint Louis Browns (43-111), the 1999 Kansas City Wizards (8 -24), the 2003 Detroit Tigers (43 – 119) and the 2008 Detroit Lions (0 – 16). Not only does history mark successful athletic teams, it also provides examples of businesses that are known for their Team Unity. Google, Inc.; Apple Inc. and CFA Properties Incorporated's, Chick-fil-A are referenced as several businesses having great team unity and resulting success.

Introduction

Dave Ramsey, bestselling author and world known financial advisor said, "When I started this company, I didn't want any employees. I still don't. Instead, I've got a great team of people who are passionate about our company mission!" As I researched these successful and unsuccessful teams, one aspect became very clear to me: A team was only as "good" or "bad" or as "successful" or "unsuccessful" as its Team Unity is.

Teams with strong Team Unity were very successful. Articles on the successful teams referenced above speak of how teammates cared for one another, upheld the values of the team and facilitated an atmosphere of encouragement and support. Conversely, teams with a lack of Team Unity were unsuccessful.

Introduction

Characteristics of these teams were dynamically different than those of successful teams. There were references to inner-team fighting, finger pointing, blaming losses on teammates and self-focused team members just to reference a few. So, how was strong Team Unity established in the successful teams and what was the cause of the lack of Team Unity in the unsuccessful ones?

It is not always the team with the most talent that wins. Let me repeat that: it is not always the team with the most talent that wins. Instead, it is most often the team where the members learned how to value and care deeply for one another, are committed to the shared goal and play well together, for each other, that wins. Team Unity is a critical component of every team's success.

Introduction

It does not matter if it is a sports team, a marriage partnership or a business team. The team must have "true" unity and cohesiveness in order for it to achieve success and accomplish its goals. The greater the level of unity achieved by a given team, the greater the level of success that team will have.

One thing is certain, only a positive result can come out of having Team Unity. Building Team Unity can be a difficult issue for any team. Many teams are not sure what "True Team Unity" is or how to go about achieving, developing or maintaining it. Many things inhibit true Team Unity from occurring such as personal goals, self-focus, lack of confidence and trust and many more.

Introduction

No matter how talented one individual player may be, any time he/she undermines team unity, it causes the whole team to suffer. Coach John Wooden wrote in his book, "Wooden on Leadership", "The star of the team is the team; 'we' supersedes 'me'", and, "it takes 10 hands to score a basket".

He further stated that any threat to Team Unity must be dealt with and done so immediately. Team Unity is so critical that any time a threat to it arises it must be addressed and eliminated at once.

TURNING SILVER INTO GOLD is designed to be an impactful, schedule sensitive read to accommodate the busy timetable, lives and agendas of all coaches, CEO's, athletes, administrators and the like.

Introduction

The contents of this book will help you understand what Team Unity is, how to develop, achieve and maintain this lifeblood of success for your team and understand the value of Team Unity.

Through reading TURNING SILVER INTO GOLD, you will gain a clear revelation into the things that prevent and destroy Team Unity and an understanding that, as you remove these threats and guard against them entering or re-entering your team, true Team Unity will be achieved. Whether you are a coach or an athlete, a leader or member of any group functioning on collaborative efforts, you will find within these pages, tools to assist you in achieving your entity's goals.

- Mike Martin

PART 1

UNDERSTANDING TEAM UNITY

1
Team Unity Defined

Team Unity in its simplest form is defined as the reflection of the whole team becoming one. The dictionary defines unity as "the state of being one; the whole or totality combining all its parts into one; an absence of diversity and oneness of mind". Unity perfected = becoming one. James (Doc) Counsilman, US Olympic and Indiana University swimming coach said this about unity: "Develop a state of mind that will concern itself with everyone on the team. If you do this you will have more than your share of champions, and fewer of these champions will have a distorted view of their own importance."

Team Unity Defined

Imagine the size, in terms of a force, that a team presents itself as having to an opponent when they present themselves with an achieved state of unity; they appear huge! As unity is achieved, again defined as the whole team becoming one, the team begins to bare real fruit in the form of success. This is because the team is reflecting the combined commitment of the team members to each other and the goals of the team. When a team is truly unified, the impossible becomes possible. The following is a great example of this.

Herman Ostry, a farmer in Bruno, Nebraska and son Mike, owned land containing a large barn that sat near a creek.

Team Unity Defined

This barn was located on a low portion of the land and was always muddy and non-functional. In 1988 there was a flood that left over 29 inches of water in the barn leaving the structure unusable. Ostry needed the barn to be functional for the purpose it was constructed. So, Herman Ostry and his son Mike decided they needed to move the 20,000-pound barn to higher ground, but from a cost standpoint, it was impossible. So they came up with a plan to enlist the assistance of their friends and community to band together and unite for a common purpose- to move their barn.

Their vision was to construct a lift system that would allow 350 people to position themselves in and around the perimeter of the barn.

Team Unity Defined

Each position/person would lift 57 pounds. Herman and Mike theorized that if each position and person lifted that amount and moved in unity, the barn could be moved.

On July 30 1988, they assembled the volunteers together, shared the need (*vision*) of moving the 20,000-pound barn 115 feet from where it sat and means of accomplishing the goal by carrying the barn to the new spot. They asked for a commitment from the 350 volunteers to each lift *57* pounds of the barn and move; at the same time.

Team Unity Defined

On the day of the move Ostry found that in addition to his 350 volunteers, there were approximately 4,000 spectators who came to watch and to see if this impossible goal could become possible. Ostry, with the help of a loud speaker, acted the part of the coach and spoke words of encouragement to the volunteers. He repeated to the team what their goal was and assured them they were going to accomplish it.

Shortly after 11:00 AM, the volunteers took up their positions and Ostry gave them one last blast of encouragement. He then, gave his first directive: "Everyone grab hold and lift." In one steady and gentle motion, the 10 ton barn lifted off the ground. Next another directive was given by Ostry: "Very slowly and very steadily, come forward."

Team Unity Defined

The barn appeared to be moving with ease. He continued to encourage his team assuring them they were doing great and were setting a great example to many as to what can be accomplished by working together.

Partway through the move, Ostry, the coach, asked his team if they felt they needed to stop and rest to regain their strength. The answer was a resounding, "No!"

The team members were fueled with energy that resulted from their commitment to the shared goal. With continued leadership and encouragement from their coach, the team lifted and moved the barn to its new home.

Team Unity Defined

This "team" was comprised of 350 diverse individuals, all with varying levels of skill, age, strength and personal interests. They were willing to look past the things that could limit them, lay aside any personal agenda and sacrifice as needed to achieve unity. Out of this Unity, they achieved a state of being "great" that day. They realized they didn't have to be the strongest, the youngest or the most physically able group of individuals in order to achieve their goal of moving the barn.

It took everyone on this team giving their best in that given moment and working together for the accomplishment of the goal for success to be achieved in the fashion it was. What was impossible became possible because of unity within the team.

Team Unity Defined

There never was any doubt in the minds of the volunteers that they would achieve their goal of moving the barn.

The thought of a goal being impossible is often the result of a person going to go at it alone; fear sets in. But reality is, a goal is only possible when it is accomplished as a team. Studies have shown that when a team is truly unified, the effect is the combined power of the team increases 5 times! This is the effect of unity!

Unity *is* "team". "Team" is achieved by unity. It is a group of diverse individuals coming together and playing or participating with a spirit of cooperation and collaboration, working towards a common goal and overcoming anything and everything that gets in the

Team Unity Defined

way of attaining that goal. Meaning, an individual seizes the opportunity to come together as a member of a team and agrees to work collaboratively with the other members for the benefit of the team. The team must be made up of a group of individuals **individually** submitted to one another.

Team Unity is an expression of interdependence. It will only work if "it" (team unity) is in first place; meaning, achieving team unity must be the priority of the team. Team members have to have the realization and mindset that each member of the team belongs to [me] and [I] belong to them. A team that cooperates and submits to one another and works together for the good of the whole, (the many that make up the team) experiences Unity.

Team Unity Defined

John Wooden used to say, "Cooperation is sacrificing for someone else's benefit. If what you are doing does not help <u>everyone involved</u>, then it is something other than cooperation, perhaps you would call it ministry, service or selfishness."

Once team members understand that every person on the team counts, that everyone can and must make a contribution and no one is superior to anyone else, then Unity exists and it exists in a manner that is fierce and powerful. The individuals put the teams' welfare ahead of his or her personal interests. As John Wooden put it, "The Star of the team **is** the team." – *My Personal Best, John Wooden*. No team is successful when it is comprised of individuals who are only concerned with their personal interests and accomplishments.

Team Unity Defined

Others and the success of the whole must be more important and held in higher regard than any personal accomplishment or attainment.

An approach and foundation that John Wooden shaped his life by is fitting to include at this point. Wooden lived by and taught the following:

> "Talent is God Given,
> Be Humble.
> Fame is Man Given,
> Be Grateful.
> Conceit is Self-Given,
> Be Careful".

Team Unity Defined

Wooden also added, "Be More Concerned with Your Character than with Your Reputation. Because Your Character Is *What* You Really Are and Your Reputation Is Merely What Others *Think* You Are."

Which do you find yourself more concerned with in life: Your Character or your Reputation? Out of that, what impact are you having on the unity of the team you are a part of?

PART 2

THE MEANS TO ACHIEVING TEAM UNITY

2
HAVING ONE VISION

Teams comprised of members that seek to focus on their individualized part of the team (concerned about self) seem to be less successful than teams that harness the combined talents and efforts of the members (concerned about the good of the team). In team unity, a leader is seeking to build a "whole" team that together will exceed the sum of its individual parts. This "whole" solidifies the unity by having a shared vision and a shared mission. Why is a shared vision (one vision) an important aspect of solidifying team unity?

Having One Vision

Les Beauchamp, Lead Pastor and Point-Person of Lifegate Church in Omaha, Nebraska, teaches "when there are two visions competing against each other within a team or organization, it is called division (di-vision). When left unchecked, division brings destruction to churches, athletic teams, business teams, businesses and homes." Another word for division is disunion.

Such would be the reason as to why shared vision is an important aspect of solidifying team unity. It is human nature to want to fulfill one's own personal goals and agendas; we all have a drive for personal achievement in life. Individuality and Unity are normally incompatible or inconsistent with each other.

Having One Vision

Individuality is a cancer to team unity. Unity is having One Vision and not Division. Division within a team is signified by the members participating and belonging with the focus on themselves, their performance, their significance and the accomplishment of their individual goals. Division within a team results in apathy and a lack of passion; an "I don't care...I'm here for myself" attitude and approach by team members.

One Vision helps a team guard against internal and external threats coming against the unity and knocking the team off the course set by the goal. Get off course and any chance of achieving the goal is gone. There generally is not enough season or time in the month left to recover, get back on course and still accomplish the goal.

Having One Vision

It is never too late to achieve unity, but it is difficult to re-establish it once it has been lost. Division on a team is like a plane that has a jumbo jet engine under one wing and a prop engine under the other.

It is going to spin out of control unable to travel in the path necessary to achieve the goal of reaching its destination. The jumbo jet engine will work to overpower the prop engine. The prop engine will cut people, wounding and injuring people in the path. Wounds defeat and prevent One Vision on a team (covered in more detail in a later chapter). The result of division will be an internal struggle by team members and the damage caused to unity will be easily seen by those who observe the team trying to function.

Having One Vision

The presence of one vision within a team produces many beneficial properties. The first is that One Vision breeds and releases passion. Passion is the fuel that keeps a team moving toward the accomplishment of the shared goal; it produces motivation. Having one vision gives direction and acts as a compass for a team. It lets a team know, "Here is the goal is there and this is the direction needed to take to achieve the goal".

Having One Vision provides a team clarity. How can a team expect to successfully achieve a goal if they don't know what they are to do or how to accomplish it? Clarity provides the team with a defined purpose, "this is what we are going after together."

Having One Vision

The goal is clearly seen by all. One Vision erases any ambiguity over purpose and what the goal is. It erases the things that would cloud or distort the view of the goal.

To help understand this, consider the image of a competitive archer. He or she must have clarity of his or her target when trying to place an arrow in a 12 centimeter circle from a distance of nearly 80 yards. Is the archer going to trust their score (their success) to chance or are they going to ensure they have clarity in acquiring their target? Clarity breaks down the goal into steps by establishing the processes and procedures necessary for achieving the coveted bullseye; the goal.

Having One Vision

The focus shifts to the level of effort needed and given towards perfecting the processes and not so much on the result of the effort. The underlying belief is that an individual is giving his or her best, the goal will be achieved. In team sports, this same principal also applies. The by-product of giving one's best is that it often results in an outcome that exceeds any given expectations or what people would label the individual or team as being able to accomplish.

The presence of One Vision for a team also produces Energy for the whole team and for individual team members. Energy and excitement is generated as a result of the realization that the individual team members are important and have something to offer to the team in assisting in achieving the shared goal.

Having One Vision

This in turn leads to "intent" by the team members. John Wooden had a great perspective on what it meant to be an athlete with intent when he said, "An intent person [athlete] will stay the course and go the distance. He or she will concentrate on objectives [shared goal] with determination, stamina and resolve. Intentness is the quality that won't permit us to quit, even when our goal is going to take a while to accomplish". – *The Greatest Coach Ever: Timeless Wisdom and Insights of John Wooden.*

Quitting is **never** an option. The energy a team produces by having One Vision fuels the team to stay in the pursuit of the shared goal the entire season or the

Having One Vision

entire fiscal period. Achieving the goal takes time; it is a marathon and not a sprint.

One Vision on a team also produces Purity. The reference here is Purity in an athlete's or team member's efforts, thoughts and offerings to the team and the results that are achieved thereby. It is impossible to turn a negative thought into a positive result or action. For example, a basketball player playing defense with the thought bubble present that says to him or herself, "I can't get beat inside again; I always get beat to the inside- I'm just not good at defending that." Chances are they are going to get beat to the inside because they're trying to take a negative thought and turn it into a positive result.

Having One Vision

They are placing their focus on a negative situation or thought during competition; that will not be productive. Purity brings about with it, a positive thought which will yield a positive result. An example is, "This is my area on the court and I am going to defend it with great resolve and determination for the good of my team. I will give all I have each and every play to keep the ball and the opponent from advancing past this area and reaching their goal." They rehearse, "This is for my team, my teammates matter to me and together we have a resolve to fight."

Comments by team captains and team leaders are critical to a team's morale and the ability for team members to give of their talent, effort and thoughts with

Having One Vision

purity. Typically, if leaders are positive, positive behaviors follow by the team members. Likewise, when leaders are negative teams will usually perform in a negative manner.

When the offering and effort the team member is giving to and for the team is pure, it speaks to teammates that he or she is reliable. Teammates can count on him or her and as a result, trust is established between team members and within the team. Unity is achieved by each member of a team understanding that "Each day should be made to be, A Masterpiece." – *The Greatest Coach Ever: Timeless Wisdom and Insights of John Wooden.* If you want to establish unity then business leaders, team leaders and coaches need to sow the seeds of positive influence in their leadership, so that

Having One Vision

these seeds reproduce themselves within the program or team. Fact: Seeds have no expiration date. They never die and when placed in the right soil, they will bear great fruit and produce a harvest.

Any athlete or business person is only able to give up to a maximum of 100% effort in a given day; that is all one is capable of producing and giving as a human being. There is no way to increase the capacity of what we are able to humanly and physically give.

We cannot give 115% or 120%. The Maximum potential of any one person toward any one team is 100%. Today only exists for today; it is finite and will end after a 24 hour period. One cannot bring it back so give all to the

Having One Vision

whole of the team while today is still today. Once it (today) occurs, it is in the past. Things done in today cannot be gone back to when tomorrow comes and be changed or made up for.

A person only has today to give his or her best; there is no borrowed time or second chance at today. One cannot give 80% today because of adverse circumstances and then plan to give 120% tomorrow to make up for it. Whatever effort level a team member gives to the team that day is left on the respective playing field for good. Whatever percentage of effort level a person does not give toward the team is lost for good. It is not stored-up nor placed in a holding tank to use at some other time. Unity is rising above the circumstances in our lives and overcoming daily

Having One Vision

obstacles, thus being able to give the full 100% each person is capable of giving to the team for the good of the whole team. Being unified Under One Vision allows for each team member to successfully do this each day for their team.

3
SACRIFICE

Team Unity is much like the principle that a leader does not become a leader because one declares him or herself to be a leader. Team Unity is not achieved merely by proclaiming that it will be a part of the culture of an athletic or business team. A coach or business leader usually is not heard saying "Isn't our team unity great? We've never worked on it, but isn't it great?" In order for Team Unity to be achieved a great deal of intentional effort must be made. It must be something that everyone involved desires to have and is committed to having; otherwise it will not be achieved.

Sacrifice

There is a price that must be paid in order for team unity to occur and be solidified.

According to the Merriam-Webster Dictionary, Sacrifice is defined as: "the surrender of something prized or desired for the sake [good] of something else." It was mentioned earlier that in order for team unity to occur, team members must be willing to sacrifice as needed. A willingness to make and endure a sacrifice comes out of and is a result of love. Love that is unconditional for ones teammates and the whole of the team is what prompts a person to willingly sacrifice. We all have images in our minds as to what sacrifice *looks like*. Perhaps the clearest example of sacrifice is the soldier sacrificing their life to save the life of a fellow soldier.

Sacrifice

The Bible says in John 15:13 that, "Greater love has no one than this: to lay down one's own life for one's friend."

Another example of sacrifice is an act of being a good Samaritan by fetching someone's car for them on a sub-zero day, or a baseball/softball player hitting a pop-fly knowing he or she will be out, but willing to sacrifice their chance of getting on base in order to advance a teammate into scoring position. These are some images *of* sacrifice. Consider now what sacrifice *is* as it relates to team unity.

One way sacrifice is made is by a team member coming to grips with the fact that no team member is bigger or better than the team.

Sacrifice

Working for the good of the whole team to accomplish the group goal is more important than the individual components of the whole achieving individual goals.

John Wooden taught the principle to not worry about or focus on being "better" than someone else. Wooden taught instead that an athlete should focus on trying to be the very best he or she can be [for the ultimate benefit of the team]. *– John Wooden and Don Yaeger, A Game Plan for Life*

If a person is giving of him or herself for the good or the benefit of the whole team, no single individual is setting all the records and receiving all the attention and praise.

Sacrifice

Unity cannot be achieved unless all involved, be it business leaders, coaches or athletes, are willing to both sacrifice and suffer- to pay the cost necessary for unity to occur.

In business, sacrifice means making the tough decisions, like making a personnel change that may affect a friend, but doing it because it is the right thing for the company as a whole. The change will help the company in the achievement of its common goal and shared mission. In athletics, it means going through two-a-day practices, conditioning until physically sick and missing time with family due to practices and tournaments. It means upholding the proper on and off field behaviors so as to not cause harm to the team by tarnishing its reputation or casting the team into a negative light.

Sacrifice

Achieving Team Unity is not likened to the running of a 100 meter or 400 meter spring race. Rather, it is better aligned with the comparison to a marathon race. A marathon race takes time, effort, training, discipline and application.

Neither is achieving Team Unity an "easy path" like that of the wide road in life. The wide road has less obstacles, takes less effort to travel. It is instead, a path like that of the narrow road. It will take effort and perseverance to travel it. The narrow road is the preferred path for life with the greatest reward at the end. There are obstacles, challenges and temptations to overcome and navigate through as you travel toward the shared goal of the team, but it is worth it as the reward at the end is great.

Sacrifice

Sacrifice means there are no shortcuts to be taken by a team member; no shortcuts to success and no shortcuts to helping the team achieve the shared goal. Every member of a team goes the distance and makes a full commitment. A team's unity will only be as strong as the level of commitment and sacrifice the members of the team give to the unity. This is true from the business leader, to trainers, to coaches and to the athletes.

A good analogy to use to help drive this point is for the team to view itself as a chain that is made up of many individual links. When the unity is strong, the links are strong and the chain is one huge unbreakable whole.

Sacrifice

But, if an individual begins to take shortcuts or compromise on his or her commitment, a link in the chain is weakened. Once a chain has a link that is weak, the whole is weakened. As a result, the chain fails. The chain [team] loses its strength, its ability and its execution. It loses unity.

Each team member must see him or herself as an important link in the chain of Unity for the team. When the revelation occurs that a person is a vital link in something as important as team unity, that person will fearlessly guard that unity- there is great personal fulfillment experienced in this for everyone who is a part.

Sacrifice

Today it seems like many athletes are not willing to make a full level of commitment and sacrifice to or for the good of the team. They are willing to make basic sacrifices but are not willing to make the sacrifices that really impact the overall "good" of the team.

Take for example the use of performance enhancing drugs (PED's). These are of no benefit to a team and a team member that uses them is not presenting him or herself as a strong link in the unity chain.

Once the use of PED's is discovered (and it eventually will be), it is brought to the public light. It reflects poorly on the team as a whole, the program and the athlete him or herself.

Sacrifice

It has a very negative effect on the Team Unity that is present at that time as well. It erodes trust and reliance among team members.

My personal opinion is that the body is only capable of being able to achieve a certain level of physical and muscular development. I believe there are only two ways of reaching this potential: (1) Performance enhancing drugs which will take you to that level of obtaining maximum potential quicker, but the effects are not worth it. The use of PED's is traced to rage, cancer, mental illness, suicide and more. The effects hardly support the use of these...it is a short term gain with very long-term side effects.

Sacrifice

(2) Hard work and sacrifice. This method of achieving the body's developmental potential may take a little longer to achieve, but the reward and benefit is much greater. The risk of all the mental and physical side effects that are associated with the performance enhancing drugs are negated and the guilt or regret of taking the shortcut is eliminated.

The way of hard work and sacrifice is its own personal reward. Knowing you did it the right way for your team, leads to much greater personal satisfaction. The results and benefits of hard work and sacrifice strongly support the use of this means.

Sacrificing means doing the things that will help one become their best and help the team.

Sacrifice

Understand that doing the things that will make one the best may conflict with doing the things one would rather be doing: spending time playing a video game, giving up when times are hard or partying on a weekend. Sacrificing is a person giving up one thing for something they feel is more important or of more value. It's making the personal choices that will benefit you and your team.

The shared vision, (shared goal) is kept at the forefront and the individual team member commits to the sacrifice of making the decisions that moves him or her and their team forward in accomplishing the shared goal.

Sacrifice

The team relies on the individuals that comprise it and the individuals rely on the team. Mia Hamm gave a great example of this principle in an article she wrote for CNN.com in July 1999, "I am a member of a team and I rely on the team, I defer to it and sacrifice for it, because the team, not the individual is the ultimate champion." This depicts imparting completely selfless acts where the intention of the selfless act is for another person's or the teams benefit.

By sacrificing in order for team unity to be achieved, one is learning to lay aside ego for the good of something they have given themselves to. Sacrificing produces great qualities in an individual like perseverance, self-denial and dedication, all qualities and characteristics that bring benefit to the whole of the team and beyond.

Sacrifice

An interesting principle of sacrifice is that in so doing, personal gain is at a much higher level than if the sacrifice had not been made. It is a willingness to forfeit something for something else considered to be of more value. Sacrifice breeds commitment. It draws team members in, closer together and takes them all to the same level; it establishes consistency. Sacrifice begs the question of teammates to teammates, "What are you willing to give up for me?" It is asking of everyone, "What are you willing to give up for the sake of the team?" If an individual team member is able and willing to positively answer the aforementioned question, a sacrificial example is held up for all other members, that in turn, generates trust among team members.

Sacrifice

There are two main negative thoughts that everyone carries with them in life that are introduced at a very young age. They shape and mold much of who an individual becomes. Generally, these thoughts are suppressed into our subconscious, but they are always there, playing over and over, whether it is realized or not. These two negative thoughts are: "I don't matter" and "No one really cares about me." The act of sacrificing disproves these two main negative thoughts and erases a huge barrier to achieving Team Unity.

4
Commitment

Sacrifice by a team member shows commitment to his or her fellow teammates as well as to the team as a whole. It says that no matter what, I am committed [to you] and outside influences will not change that. Sacrifice breeds commitment. It draws team members in, closer together and takes them all to the same level; it establishes consistency and unity within the commitment.

Commitment

Commitment insulates against allowing external influences to dictate how a team member reacts or exerts them self for the good of the team in the face of those external influences.

Commitment enables a person/team member/athlete to see life from a different view point; a perspective that is different that his or hers. One's own perspective is often self-serving and limited. It can hinder what the team is trying to do as a whole.

Sometimes one's own perspective can be inspired by a false reality. A false reality is an improper analysis of data. One can be led to have a false reality just by having better sales numbers than other team members for a short period of time or an athlete having better

Commitment

statistics that his or her teammates during a season. The false reality that is produced is that the team cannot function or succeed without them. This creates a perspective that can hinder the team or worse- weave a destructive thread throughout the team.

All members of a team must be willing to find a new perspective. That is, to be able to build a perspective that is based on an accurate analysis of data. What is it that the "team" is trying to achieve? What is my role? What does the team need from me? Team members must get hooked into the flow and direction the team is going and must commit to the steps necessary for the team to achieve the goals it has set.

Commitment

Furthermore, the team member must commit to the things he or she is able to supply to the team, for the good of the team in achieving those goals. Team members have to eliminate thoughts that go against the goals of the team they are a part of.

Sacrifice and Commitment go hand-in-hand and are vital to Team Unity being "Achieved". Commitment is what allows a team member to be able to Sacrifice and Sacrifice is the manifestation of commitment. When commitment is present, a team member identifies what is needed by the team and then makes the extra effort.

He or she does more than what is asked or required of them in spite of the situation or circumstances.

Commitment

He or she produces the needed results in spite of the external forces. One cannot choose what test or external forces/influences will be faced in life, but one can certainly choose how one will respond to them.

Commitment enables a team member to give a full effort and overcome and not take shortcuts that would threaten to cause a set-back to the team. It is the Principle of Priority: Whatever your Priority is, is where all your efforts in life will go. The opposite of commitment is mere interest. Example: if one is merely "interested" in seeing the team he or she is a part of, achieve unity, it probably won't happen.

Commitment

Remember, commitment is what allows sacrifice to occur. Interest is not commitment. It could lead to commitment, but being interested in something does not equal being committed to it. If a team member is only interested in achieving unity or interested in the success of the team, he or she will only do that which is required of them; they won't go above and beyond and they won't make the necessary sacrifices required to achieve that which the team is seeking. Remember, the Principle of Priority mentioned just a few sentences ago.

So if Interest and Commitment are polar opposites, it is important to remove 'interest' in team members' minds and convert it to commitment.

Commitment

Interest will create dissention, conflict and behavior problems both on and off the field of play; it is a recipe for the destruction of a team. Interest means no commitment. No commitment means, no sacrifice.

5
Self-LESS-ness

Giving of one's self effort, talents and abilities for the good of the team can only be done with effectiveness if they are <u>given with nothing expected in return.</u> As denoted by the spelling of this chapter's title, it involves *less* of one's self focus and conversely, an increase in the focus on others. Unity is achieved by the unselfish giving of "self" to the good of the team. Giving must be done self-**less**-ly.

Self-LESS-ness

When a high school athlete commits to a university, on signing day he or she must take on the mindset that they are becoming a part of a "team" and that they are bringing their abilities and talents to the team for the good of the team. Likewise, when a company hires a new employee that person must come into the company with the same mindset and understanding that the athlete does when joining a team.

Selflessness within athletes appears to be a dying character trait in today's athletic world. A trend is developing in the college level, where after one or two seasons, an athlete voices they are not happy with the way things are going for them and that they are looking to transfer.

Self-LESS-ness

They think they should be playing more, should be playing ahead of another team member at the same position and should be given more opportunity.

When I played college football in the mid 1980's, athletes usually spent the first two years on the practice team, learning plays, pushing starters to get better and helping the team get ready to play. They spent time in the weight room and developing skills, and then followed by earning playing time in their last two years. Today, many athletes are coming out of high school with an expectation that they are going to be a starter in their given sport their freshman year in college; this is unrealistic.

Self-LESS-ness

Coming to a school with unrealistic expectations and a self-focused mindset is not an example of a Self-LESS athlete. An athlete must trust in the coaches that they are making the decisions that are best for the team as far as who plays where and when.

This does not mean that an athlete should not have personal goals or should not seek to experience success in making personal improvements or obtaining personal accomplishments. The fundamental guiding principle here is that personal goals have a place in achieving team unity. How? By ensuring personal goals are designed to make the individual better, which in turn, will help the team achieve its common goal.

Self-LESS-ness

Consider a football team setting a common goal of winning three more games next season. The starting running back sets a personal goal of setting a new squatting personal best in the weight room over winter conditioning. He has shared this goal with his teammates.

Throughout winter conditioning his teammates have been encouraging him, charting and celebrating strength gains. Together they have been working toward the achievement of his personal goal. Together they know that if the running back achieves his personal goal, he will be faster and more agile resulting in more rushing yards each game in the upcoming season. More yards per game means a greater likelihood of more points scored.

Self-LESS-ness

More points scored each game means a greater likelihood of the team achieving its common goal of winning three more games next season. The running back may very well receive awards and recognition for his performance, but the awards are a fruit of the effort and focus being placed on the good of the whole team.

In kind, a basketball team has a common goal of improving its perimeter shooting percentage. The team realizes that in order to do this, they must have an action step of improving its performance in screen setting. Better screen setting will ultimately provide better shots on the perimeter which will result in the accomplishment of the shared goal.

Self-LESS-ness

Team members must realize that their role as the person setting the screen is equally as important and valuable as the person who will be shooting on the perimeter. Everyone must commit to working on his or her screen setting skills for the good of the team.

This may well mean that scoring averages for some may go down because they are spending more time setting highly effective screens, but to them it is worth it because of the good it will yield for the team. A self-LESS team member in athletics or business does not concern him or herself with the "WIIFM Factor"; the "What's In It For Me" factor.

Self-LESS-ness

They are not worried about if they will be the starter, score the most points, get the headlines and cheers...they are concerned with what is best for the team on any given day, at any given moment. They are concerning themselves with thoughts of how they can best help the team and how they can help teammates excel.

Self-LESS athletes (and business people) have a firm understanding of the principle that the name on the front of the uniform is much more important than the name or number on the back. That is, it is more important that the "team" and the "entity" represented on the front of the jersey do well that day vs. the person wearing the jersey (their name on back) doing well.

Self-LESS-ness

It is exactly the application of the principal where the whole is more important to the individual than the individual is to him or herself and his or her personal success; he or she holds the team's success in higher standing than the importance of his or her own personal success.

Self-LESS athletes not only look for ways to serve their team, they also look for ways in which they can impact those they are playing or competing against. They tend to play with greater sportsmanship and character. They play clean, assist a fallen opponent up or tend to them when seriously injured. The presence of a self-LESS athlete will many times cause the level of play in a given competition to come to a higher and more respectable level.

Self-LESS-ness

In many cases, when self-LESS athletes are involved in a game, there are fewer penalties called, fewer injuries and less fights break out. Often, self-LESS athletes leave those they play with and against, feeling valued and having been positively impacted.

The same is true in business. When others are around or working with Self-Less business leaders or associates, they often come away realizing they have been positively impacted by that experience.

The self-LESS athlete embraces teammates in celebrating his or her accomplishments on the field. They realize that the accomplishment was not possible without all of the parts working together; it takes everyone on the team to be able to succeed.

Self-LESS-ness

This goes even farther. True self-LESS athletes will often celebrate an accomplishment as a unit and then turn towards the sidelines, to embrace and celebrate with the rest of the team. They know that the celebration is not complete until the team has celebrated as a whole.

When a team has self-focused team members, there is a stark and very noticeable difference from what is described above. When something great happens on a team of self-focused athletes, you don't see the team or unit coming together to celebrate. Instead, when the camera zooms in on a self-focused athlete after a big catch for a touchdown, or a goal scored in an intense soccer match or the winning shot in a final four showdown, you see something very different.

Self-LESS-ness

You see the athlete celebrating "self" (the individuals name or number on the back of the jersey) instead of celebrating "team" (the name of the team on the front of the jersey). They celebrate themselves and make it "their big play" instead of the team's big play and accomplishment together. The athlete will literally push away teammates who have run up to him or her to celebrate together in order to allow for the call for the applause and approval of the crowd and ensure the camera is solely on them. They will extend their arms in greatness, while continuing to make the effort to remain separated from teammates that come up to celebrate.

Self-LESS-ness

The following scenario played out last fall in a prime-time football game: A touchdown was scored on a play that had great individual effort by a running back. However, an even greater team effort occurred by those blocking and assisting the running back. After the touchdown, a teammate immediately came running up to celebrate. The running back that carried the ball into the end zone held the ball out in his right arm and extended his left arm out to push away the teammate. He proceeded to run the width of the end zone pushing teammate after teammate away, celebrating only himself.

Soon, he found himself alone in the corner of the end zone, having finished calling for the praise of the fans for "his" accomplishment.

Self-LESS-ness

His teammates got tired of trying to celebrate <u>with</u> him what <u>they</u> had accomplished together, so they went and celebrated together as a unit away from him and then headed to the sideline to celebrate with the rest of their teammates. Not long thereafter, the camera showed the running back on the sideline bench. He was sitting alone, no one was around him. He had displayed to his team that he cared only about himself and was committed to his personal performance and accomplishments only.

If there was much team unity on that team, what does these types of actions do to it? Individuality on a team will **always** either destroy the unity that is present or prevent it from occurring in the first place.

Self-LESS-ness

In order for true success to be achieved on a team, "self" must be laid aside and "team" must be embraced and made the priority.

When an athlete (team member) pushes teammates away or moves away from them in order to celebrate "self" and infers to them, "No thanks, this is my moment to highlight 'me' and what I've done", it erodes any and all unity. These actions create a culture of independence; a culture of individualism. This will destroy a team and will make it difficult to rebuild or reestablish unity on the team for a long period of time. Individualism, which is the opposite of self-LESS-ness, reduces loyalty and mutual trust amongst a team.

Self-LESS-ness

A study by Baylor University revealed that individualists are motivated by what is good for them personally, are independent and self-reliant. This is counter intuitive to the mindset of a self-LESS member of a team who puts the team first, prioritizes what is good for the team over what is good for self and seeks to have the best for the team be the result of his or her participation on the team.

According to Tom Osborne, one of the greatest coaches in college football history, there are a few key ingredients in order to have a great team. In Osborne's book, Faith In the Game, he states, "In order to have a great team, there must be a great deal of loyalty, mutual trust and genuine caring and love [by teammates] for other teammates."

Self-LESS-ness

Coach Osborne talks frequently in books and interviews about the tremendous amount of Team Unity his 1994, 1995 and 1997 National Championship teams had. He talks of how they cared for each other, sacrificed for the good of the team and how they gave of themselves and their talents for the team. So, when a teammate is only interested in his or her own accomplishments and celebrating only him or herself, it causes the rest of the team to question and doubt them. It causes them to ask, "Are you as committed to (dependent on) me as I am to you?" It makes sense, after all, they have given blood, sweat, sacrifice and tears together for what they thought was for the common goal of and benefit of the team.

Self-LESS-ness

A great anonymous quote (often attributed to President Truman, John Wooden and Blanton Collier) reads, "It is amazing what a team can accomplish if they do not worry about who is getting the credit". Foster self-LESS-ness among team members and manage, coach out and coach up a mindset of individualism. With an atmosphere of self-LESS-ness the team can accomplish more than anyone imagined.

Allow individualism and the team will constantly struggle and performance, along with results, will be on a continual decline. This is true in athletics and business. When a person has a sole focus of promoting themselves, it creates a barrier between team members. This barrier leads to an obvious state of disunity. Here is an example of how it commonly appears.

Self-LESS-ness

Often "camps" arise. Camps are groups of members of a team that side up with other members. They either align with the individualist, thus supporting their actions, or they join together with others who recognize and reject the ill effects of individualism on a team. In a synergistic effort, they try to preserve any remaining unity that exists on the team.

Individualism on any team is like a cancer is to the human body. It must be identified where individualism lies within the team. How advanced or how much of a threat to the team the individualism is must be assessed and then the individualism must be removed with the surgical precision and accuracy that cancer is removed from the body.

Self-LESS-ness

If a cancer is left unaddressed in the human body, it will continually attack the body, tear it down, weaken it, compromise its performance and will eventually cause the death of the body. When individualism is left unaddressed on a team, it will continually attack the team, tear it down, weaken it, compromise its performance and will eventually cause the death of the team.

6
Character and Integrity

Character and Integrity play a huge part in achieving Team Unity. The dictionary defines character as a moral or ethical quality; qualities of honesty, courage. It also defines it as a person's reputation. It is said that character is doing the right thing; even when nobody is watching. Integrity is defined as an adherence to moral and ethical principles and of being of unimpaired condition. These are important threads of achieving Team Unity as they are foundational building blocks.

Character and Integrity

As a team establishes a shared common goal, a code of behavior is also established. It is the team member's individual level of character and integrity that drives commitment to the goal and to the code of behavior. The question is will one [will we] compromise on their [our] integrity when faced with a temptation or will they [will we] hold true to their [our] commitment to the goal and the team? Who an individual is as a person is far more important than who the individual is as an athlete or business person.

When integrity prevails, a team will less likely face behaviors that are demeaning to the team or the entity/institution, be it on or off the respective field of play. Integrity means that your "yes" is your "yes".

Character and Integrity

If a commitment by a team member is made to the team, the team knows, because of the team member's integrity, that he or she will uphold that commitment.

A good example of this is a story John Wooden tells in his book, *My Personal Best* when he was a finalist for the head coaching job at both the University of Minnesota and UCLA. A major snowstorm in Minneapolis made it impossible for the University of Minnesota to reach Wooden with a job offer. That same day Minnesota was trying to call to offer him the job, UCLA was also trying to reach Coach Wooden to offer him the head coaching job.

The call from UCLA got through and since he had not received a call from Minnesota, he accepted.

Character and Integrity

Phone service was restored in the Minneapolis area fifteen minutes after Coach Wooden accepted the UCLA job. Minnesota continued their efforts to reach Wooden to offer him the job. When they finally did reach him, Coach Wooden was faced with a dilemma.

The Minnesota job was Wooden's personal preference but he had already accepted the job offered to him by UCLA. Even though Minnesota was inundated by an April blizzard, the integrity Wooden operated upon in his life dictated that he honor the commitment he made to UCLA by verbally accepting their offer. The rest, as they say, is history. The success both Wooden and UCLA experienced during the time he was head coach of the men's basketball program was the result of his integrity filled answer.

Character and Integrity

One way in which character is formed is by the friends that one keeps and the people one surrounds them self with from the start to finish of life. Friends often predict the direction ones future will take.

Studies show that a person will often become like the friends they associate with. Keep bad friends and it is likely one will make bad or poor choices which will most likely lead to destructive behaviors; destructive personally, destructive to others and destructive to a team.

People tend to surround themselves with friends that make them feel good about them self. They often do this when they are making bad decisions, participating in destructive behaviors.

Character and Integrity

People surround them self with friends that don't call them out on it, don't question why they are doing what they are doing. This means [I/they] don't have to deal with the pain, hurt and shame associated with poor decisions. People often become defensive to anyone who challenges them on their poor behavior and poor decisions.

Defensiveness means a person will not validate the way someone is feeling about how they are behaving (even though they may be right). Furthermore it means they will not give thought or consideration to the chance that they may be part of the problem. Instead, the person making the bad decisions says, "I think you are the problem" to the person who is trying to point something

Character and Integrity

out or help. This destroys intimacy and prevents commitment, loyalty and honesty.

Earlier, it was shown how important intimacy, commitment, loyalty and honesty are to being able to achieve true team unity. It is better for everyone for a person to surround them self with friends that compel them and challenge them to do the right thing and do things for the good of others.

If people surround themselves with friends that drive them toward doing the right thing, making right choices and non-destructive behaviors, they will develop stronger character. A benefit of having friends like this is that accountability can be established.

Character and Integrity

Accountability is a discipline of practice that allows one's self to be held responsible to someone for one's actions, thoughts and behaviors.

It is giving a close group of friends the right to ask the tough questions, to challenge on behaviors and the path one is on and also encourage them along. There is a misconception that being accountable to others is a sign of weakness. Nothing could be farther from the truth. In fact, being accountable to others is more a sign of wisdom and strength. A leader should challenge them self and decide to be the one who is the influencer (on others in a good way) instead of being the one influenced (by others in a negative way). A leader should also be the one to challenge the team to pick friends of good quality and character and surround

Character and Integrity

them self with them and to tell the "bad" friends they simply cannot be friends with them anymore; and, if they tell them why they are choosing not to be friends anymore; now that will be influence!

Character must be consistent. That is, a person should be consistent in his or her character no matter whom he or she is around. Many times character and behavior is changed to match that of the character and behavior of a given group one is with. In so doing, a person becomes like a palm tree. A palm tree has no structure, no rigidity. It is blown by whatever direction the wind is blowing and its behaviors and actions are governed by an external force. A person who allows his or her character to match that of those who he or she is with is in kind, being shaped by an external force.

Character and Integrity

Consistency in character says that no matter the circumstances or environment in which one is in, one will be who one really is; one's walk and one's talk will match up and will align. Integrity reinforces the decision to honor one's character. Compromised integrity leaves a person vulnerable to the negative influences of his or her environment.

Once compromise occurs, it is difficult to regain the ability to stand up to the negative influences and it is difficult to become the influencer once again. The importance of character and integrity, when it comes to Team Unity is that it allows a team to trust each other.

Character and Integrity

A team being able to trust one another leads to loyalty and honoring *of* one another and *to* one another, a preferring of teammates over self and as a result, a ferocity in achieving a shared goal; the execution of team unity. If compromise occurs within a team, it erodes trust and makes it difficult for the team to reestablish this important component of team unity.

Character and Integrity are often produced by way of suffering. It is through suffering that character is often developed. Character reveals who a person is at their core. The only way to demonstrate a person's character, (who a person is at the core) is to live an honest and open life. That is, live as an "Aggregate Person". What is an aggregate person? Liken it to an aggregate fruit.

Character and Integrity

For example, a strawberry is an aggregate fruit because it has seeds and you can see them. The aggregate of one's traits and features tell people who someone is. No one has to tell a person who they are because what is inside of them will be seen.

There is benefit to the ideas that suffering produces character. It sets the tone for the team and it develops quality leadership within it. A leader sets the expectation of what others behaviors, goals etc. will be. A leader leads by servanthood and example. A good leader will never ask anyone to do something he/she would not do or has not done. Leadership demands character. Followers must have trust in their leader.

Character and Integrity

Santa Clara University, along with the Tom Peters Group, did a study on the traits of leadership. Some of the top ones were as follows: honesty, competency, forward-looking, inspiring, intelligent and courageous.

Aggregate traits should, at the end of the day, match up with and stand for all of what an individual (a leader) stands for. Actions speak louder than words. The tongue is an overflow of the heart so what one does and what one says is the reflection of who one is. Most anyone can go through adversity and "make it" in some form or fashion, but character is truly seen in how one handles success.

Character and Integrity

The Character and Integrity that is produced by and refined in suffering will bring about the influence and leadership that changes the culture of a team, as well as improves behaviors and has positive influence that extends beyond just the team. It is like the tea bag and hot water. Which one is doing the influencing?

Is it the tea bag influencing the hot water or the hot water activating the tea bag and thus having influence on it? Without the influence of Character and Integrity you cannot have leadership. Without leadership there can be no Team Unity.

PART 3

THE COACHES ROLE IN ACHIEVING TEAM UNITY

7
Setting The Expectation Early On

A coach's role in his or her team achieving team unity is highly significant. In chapter 3 of this book it was noted that a coach does not usually say, "You know, we never work on our team's unity, but isn't it wonderful?" Much like a farmer prepares the field and ensures the growing conditions are optimal for their crops, a coach needs to ensure that the necessary components of and environment for achieving Team Unity are in place at all times for their teams. This starts as early on, in recruiting high school athletes or orientating a new hire.

Setting The Expectation Early On

Coaches need to evaluate the mindset of their recruits and seek out athletes with the attitudes and character traits that will foster unity on the team they are being asked to join. Coach Dabo Swinney, head football coach of the Clemson Tigers, said in a rebuttal to a compliant expressed by the Freedom from Religion Foundation, "Players of any faith or no faith at all are welcome in our program. All we require in the recruitment of any player is that he must be a great player at his position, meet the academic requirements and have good character."

Coaches should be setting the expectation in meetings they are having in the living rooms of high school recruits, with parents present, letting them know up front that the athlete is being asked to become a part of

Setting The Expectation Early On

a *team*. That is, to become a part of a group of individuals that are united, care about one another and work together for the good of the whole. They will be a part of a team made up of individuals who are willing to give their all, be patient and who are willing to sacrifice personal desires and change their focus from "self" to "team".

If the perspective athlete is able to grasp, embrace and commit to these requirements, then and only then should he/she be invited onto the team; coaches are responsible for setting the foundation for team unity to occur. A coach must be straight forward with a recruit and give them an honest delivery of what he or she can and should expect when becoming a part of the team.

Setting The Expectation Early On

Whether it is a high school athlete being recruited for a college team or a college athlete being drafted for a pro team, a clear understanding of what "reality" will be like upon joining the team should be given. If a coach is upfront with an athlete in this way, it will help the team member foster trust as a member of that team.

Too often athletes are made promises of being a superstar from day one, only to show up and be disappointed that they are second or third deep on the depth chart in their first season; this ties right into the Character and Integrity that was discussed in the previous chapter.

Setting The Expectation Early On

Making promises of success creates a sense of entitlement and you can catch any Sports Center or NFL Live show and hear them speak of how 'entitlement mentality' is a growing problem at all levels of athletics. Business leaders report that today, perspective employees are presenting with a sense of entitlement for earnings and paid time off before they have ever been offered a job or worked their first day.

Coaches need to be aware of and avoid being influenced by external forces (competitive recruiting) that cause them to make promises to an athlete they knowingly cannot deliver on. They likely are doing it only because it is what they think the athlete wants to hear and is what they believe will compel them to commit to play for their respective team.

Setting The Expectation Early On

Consistent character and integrity should say to a prospective athlete nothing more than they will be given the opportunity to compete and show their talents and abilities to the coaches. They should be told that if they grade the best, honor and compete for "the team", then they will **earn** the right to participate on the field. Every prospective athlete should be told that they will have the opportunity to develop and excel and, as a result, success *could* prove to be a reality for them.

The same principle applies in business. Every prospective employee should be told he or she will have the opportunity to show their talents, their commitment to the team and earn the chance to be promoted and advance within the organization they are a part of.

Setting The Expectation Early On

This provides a realistic understanding for them and gives them something to aspire to. It also helps with the retention of strong performing employees.

Coaches must let a prospective team member know what the members of the team he or she is being invited to join expect from each other as well: what the code of conduct is among the team, what is tolerated and what is not. Examples of current Team Unity and the successes it has brought the team should be shared. This can prove to be more powerful and compelling to a prospective team member than making promises about his or her future or the brand of athletic wear he/she will be given.

Setting The Expectation Early On

If a prospective team member is not interested in the team or the culture of the team or does not provide or ask about what he or she can bring to strengthen and make the team better, a coach or staff may want to think twice about inviting that person onto the team. An athlete that wants to come and be a part of the "team" and contribute to the "team" and be a "team member" that is founded in character and integrity will have tremendous positive impact on the overall success of the team he or she becomes a part of.

Conversely, an athlete that wants to know what is in it for him or her and what the team can do for them will have tremendous negative impact on a team and the success of that team will be greatly hampered.

Setting The Expectation Early On

In his self-authored book, "Uncommon", Tony Dungy tells of a situation where character was more important to evaluate than talent. In 1998 Dungy was coaching the Tampa Bay Buccaneers. Enter the Indianapolis Colts; a team he would be Head Coach of in the near future. The Colts that year were faced with a dilemma in the NFL Draft. They had the first pick in the NFL draft and the team needed a quarterback. The two top quarterback prospects were Ryan Leaf and Peyton Manning. Both were record setters in college and had the size and physical skills [talent] to be great players.

Colts President, Bill Polian, needed to make a decision on which one he was going to draft; a decision sure to have a lasting impact on the organization.

Setting The Expectation Early On

The Colts drafted Peyton Manning and Coach Dungy wrote in his book, "What tipped the scales in Bill's mind were Peyton's work ethic, his love for the game, his approach toward football as a job and his quiet personal life. Ultimately, when faced with the choice that would define the course of the franchise, the Colts based that decision on character."

He went on to say, "For the Colts, character is a quality that can be measured just like height, weight and speed. In fact, we put more emphasis on this area than we do on physical tools [talent]. Coaching ability or talent cannot make up for a lack of character." The character of team members and prospective team members is vital to the potential success of a given team. Strong character must be present.

Setting The Expectation Early On

For the Colts, there were only a few things that would knock a player out of consideration for them when it came to the draft, and character (or a lack thereof) was one of them. Dungy indicated the Colts had a category on their player evaluation forms called, "DNDC"- Do Not Draft because of Character. In 2002 the Colts hired Dungy as Head Coach. They were a powerhouse for many years under Coach Dungy and they were built upon character over talent. The Team's Leadership was willing to risk losing a good player in order to get one with the type of talent and team focus they wanted.

The Colts were consistent in their expectations of their team members and expressed those to them from the very onset.

Setting The Expectation Early On

There was no ambiguity among the team members as to what was important to the leadership of the team and the team itself; it was "the team".

They built their dynasty on players that were about the team's success and not personal success. They identified those potential team members that displayed the qualities and character traits they were looking for and invited them onto the team. They understood, built and protected Team Unity. As a result, they were Super Bowl Champions in 2006 and Dungy was the first African American Head Coach to win the Super Bowl.

The very process outlined above is how character is forged and developed within a team.

Setting The Expectation Early On

As a leader, one is faced with decisions and has to look at what is most important (what will benefit the team the most) and then make the right decision based on that. There are many coaches of teams of every age, on record stating they believe that character is at the center of what is necessary for an individual to be a good team player and team member.

Setting the expectation early on will give the perspective team member a clear reality of what will be expected of him or her as they progress toward joining and becoming a part of the team.

Setting The Expectation Early On

The benefit is they enter into the team with the same level of understanding and awareness of what is expected as those that are existing members of the team. Coming into a team from this perspective provides a much greater chance of success when it comes to achieving Team Unity.

8
Be A Leader Worth Following

The Head Coach, CEO, Manager or Director is ultimately the leader of the team. They are the leader because of the position of authority he or she has been placed in within the team or organization. There is really no debating this one on the part of the team members. By way of the title, the head coach carries the authority to make decisions and lead the team in the direction and the way he or she thinks is best. The team members, by way of their subordinate role, have a duty to follow that leadership. It is inherent in them to want to follow the leadership of their head coach.

Be A Leader Worth Following

A person cannot simply declare themselves to be the leader and expect others to follow them just because of that declaration. A leader must be a leader worthy of following. That is, they must earn the following of their leadership by the team and its members. So how does a leader be a leader worthy to follow? The answer: first, by lifestyle. He or she must lead in a way that motivates people, proves to them that as a leader, their best interest is always in mind and the leader is trustworthy. Trust is hard to establish but is easy to lose. This is accomplished by "Servant Leadership".

Servant Leadership means the leader is first a servant of those he or she is leading.

Be A Leader Worth Following

Others are a servant leader's priority. The servant leader doesn't see "being at the top" as equating to "having power". Instead, he or she strives to be under those they serve by caring for them and putting the needs of others above their own. This type of leadership inspires others to perform at a high level, often at levels they did not know they were personally capable of performing at. It builds trust between the leader and those they are leading.

There is also leadership provided from within the team by a member or members of the team, program or organization that is subordinate to its overall leadership. Those leaders (peer leaders) have the right to speak up, to provide direction and govern within the team.

Be A Leader Worth Following

However, every leader (be they the overall leader or a peer leader) must understand that there is a balance in leading that must exist in order for that leadership to be effective. That balance is the understanding they are *of* authority, but equally important, they are *under* authority.

A leader of a team may have an idea of a policy or procedure they feel is best for the team, or sense an area that needs to be addressed within the team. Yet, before doing so, in being under authority, he/she must understand the heart, vision and intent the head coach or executive has for the team and adhere to it.

Be A Leader Worth Following

In a show of honor to the head coach or executive, it is good practice for the peer leader to go to them with their idea or intention and seek their approval to act on it. As the leader displays this honor to and acknowledgment of being under the authority of the head coach or executive, the team members will take note and will also display the honor to and acknowledgment of being under the leadership of the leader. This helps to prevent power struggles.

Coaches model commitment to the team as a whole and model sacrifice by way of countless hours staying up watching film, evaluating team members, getting the right personnel in place and the right plays lined up to give the team the best chance it can have to compete and accomplish its shared goal.

Be A Leader Worth Following

Business leaders do this by comparing results with goals, analyzing current strategies, developing and implementing changes that benefit the team as a whole. They show commitment and sacrifice by doing the extra things that in turn, will give the team a chance to be competitive and a chance to achieve its goal.

A great leader never asks a team member to do anything that he or she hasn't done already themselves for that team. In order to lead effectively, a leader has to see himself/herself under those they lead; they have to see themselves as a servant. Others (those they serve) are placed first and the leader sees it as an honor to be second to those they serve. Servant leadership involves honoring those the leader serves. The result of dishonor is shame.

Be A Leader Worth Following

In medieval times, knights were stripped of rank and authority and a samurai warrior's hair (symbolic of them being at the top of the of the class hierarchy) was cut if they were seen to have been dishonoring. True honor is not worrying about being noticed. It is about others being noticed.

This kind of leadership compels others to follow and inspires them to achieve great results. Team members know they are valued, that they matter and that they are loved. This alone is a huge compelling force behind every team member that enables them to accomplish more than they thought or dreamed they were capable of.

Be A Leader Worth Following

Being a leader worth following means leading with consistency- one doesn't change one's ethics in order to adapt to a situation to make it easier for them. One is who one is and from that, he or she must lead consistently. It means the rules are honored, upheld and not bent. Often the character of the team matches the character of the leader. If the leader bends the rules, the team will bend the rules and in so doing, it is likely the team will be hurt by the bending of rules at a critical moment.

Being a leader worth following means one leads with fairness. That is, there are no favorites, exceptions are not made and one is able to rise above any personal prejudices toward a particular person or situation.

Be A Leader Worth Following

The thing that has set leaders apart from others over time is not that they assert themselves to some self-proclaimed level of leadership, nor do they clamor to be heard, nor do they seek a position because it is "good" for them. What sets them apart is the fact that they have an undying commitment to serve others and stand up for them. They put their money where their mouth is and put action to the words that have been spoken. There is no sense of entitlement, no self-seeking rank of power. Leaders that stand out as leaders, have for years, served those they lead by putting themselves under the team and by displaying genuine care and concern for them and about them. This in turn has produced teams that have defied the odds in business, life and athletics.

Be A Leader Worth Following

If one as a leader wants to achieve incredible results with a team and desires to see good leadership within the ranks of the team, then as the leader one has to sow seeds of leadership that it might reproduce.

It is a fact that seeds have no expiration date; they never die and when placed in the right soil, they bear fruit. The leaders job is to ensure he or she has created a 'right environment' (the soil) that is ready to receive the seeds being sown and that once those seeds are embedded in the soil- they will produce a continual harvest of genuine leadership and achievement of goals that exceeds even the wildest of imaginations! –The impossible becomes possible.

PART 4

THE RESULT OF ACHIEVING TEAM UNITY

9

THE ABSENCE OF FEAR

Fear cripples. It will paralyze an athlete or a sales professional, business leader and the like. Fear is an emotion that each person has been motivated by in their lifetime; if honest, most everyone is motivated by some form of fear today. Some have learned how to erase the crippling effects of fear yet, the majority of the population is still governed by fear. So, what is it that people are afraid of?

The Absence of Fear

The most common forms of fear are fear of failure, fear of ensuing rejection and isolation from that failure, fear of what other people's opinions are and a fear of having what it takes to measure up. Fear breeds shame and shame destroys an atmosphere of vulnerability and trust.

A team whose members are gripped by fear is like a plant that has been planted is a sealed environment, put in a dark place that is void of light. It has no life, no fruit…it had all the potential in the world but no success. The growing conditions were not right and did not even give this plant a chance. Fear is a chosen response to a situation that is yet to occur- it is based on "what if's" to a situation that is just a probability and not yet a reality.

The Absence of Fear

Yet, so many people focus on the 'what if' of a situation that is not yet a reality. They choose to make it a reality in their mind, a false reality, and thus choose to make a toxic decision; a toxic decision for them and the team- they choose fear, choose to be afraid. Fear then renders them unable to move, unable to commit to or for the team, unable to sacrifice for the team or to place the team and its goals in a place of priority.

In an environment where leadership is based on serving and placing one's self under those that are led, people quickly realize that the leader has their best interest in mind and that the leader is genuinely concerned for them, their success and the success of the team. In a culture where leadership speaks value to team members, fear is erased.

The Absence of Fear

As a leader, one has to lay aside and turn away from the mindset of the old style drill sergeant. The leader who stands and barks out commands and then delights in belittling and ridiculing everyone who fails, in front of others is an ineffective leader. Their role as a leader will be short-lived because no one will be willing to follow them. Remember, people will only follow the leadership of someone they feel is worth following. The military has changed their approach to the role of the drill sergeant. It used to be that he or she would stand over new enlistees at basic training and break them down, ridicule them and see how many new members of the unit they could get to quit. They would belittle these individuals in the presence of their peers and highlight their failures.

The Absence of Fear

Today's drill sergeants make it a priority to develop a strong solider physically, but they place greater effort on teaching soldiers to be, that they need each other. That their fellow brother or sister soldier is more important than they are and that no matter what, even if it means harm to themselves, protecting their fellow soldier is priority. <u>That</u> is erasing fear, making a commitment, being willing to sacrifice, and thus achieving Team Unity!

Part of being a good leader is the ability to take risks. In order to take a risk, a leader must effectively overcome and eliminate fear. A leader must see the value in taking the risk of a different approach to leadership than the old style drill sergeant.

The Absence of Fear

He or she must be willing to take the risk of allowing them self to value team members, become genuinely concerned for them and about them. Take the risk allowing them, as a leader, to express unconditional acceptance and encouragement toward team members.

When failure comes, the leader must take a risk and consider building up the team member that failed in the presence of his or her peers, expressing how valuable they are to the team; build them up, not tear them down. This will help team members to care about each other because they see the leader caring about the team and its members.

The Absence of Fear

Those being led will adopt that attitude and approach and will subsequently care about the members in the same way, if not stronger, because they are the ones battling together. They are the ones that must commit to the common objective and goal and then be willing to sacrifice in order to achieve it. If a leader can build a team that is bonded in and by love, they will have a team that will battle more courageously, with more ferocity and will overcome barriers and defy the odds.

The sense of worth of the team members cannot be wrapped up in their performance. They have to understand that they belong, are wanted, are important and matter. When love exists, fear is erased and the crippling effects of it are eliminated. Love leads others to believe, "I can", fear speaks convincingly, "you can't".

The Absence of Fear

The unity of a team built out of love empowers a team to overcome in the face of adversity, to keep a level head in times of trouble and to draw strength from the love for the teammates and rise above. A bond is forged among the team that is not easily broken. It is important that every team be given the opportunity and ability to fight and compete. When fear is present, that ability is stripped from a team. That is why talented teams are seen struggling week in and week out to meet a goal or achieve a victory.

PART 5

PROTECTING TEAM UNITY

10

Eliminating the Threats

In order to protect team unity, we must understand what threatens it. Throughout the chapters of this book I have outlined those things; they are:

- Division within the team
- Lack of willingness to sacrifice for the team
- Being a selfish team member
- The absence of character and integrity
- A lack of knowledge of expectations
- Being a leader not worthy of following
- The existence of fear in team members

Eliminating The Threats

These are all real threats to team unity ever being established and serve as dangerous threats to team unity once it has been established.

Another way in which team unity is threatened is in the locker room, gatherings and get togethers. It only takes one statement that attacks the character of a team member to begin to strip away at the bond of team unity. It is like putting hydrochloric acid on a raw material. It will slowly eat away at the material, strip it down of its core make up and eventually, eliminate its existence. It is important that the team leadership and team member **praise** more than they **criticize.**

Eliminating The Threats

Praise from other team members will build up self-esteem. Criticism will reintroduce fear into the member(s) of team. This is "peer-influence". Peer influence is huge in protecting team unity. When a team is able to self-police the culture of the team and is able to identify and deal with threats to unity, tranquility is achieved in the realm of unity and what it will produce for a team is immeasurable. One of the greatest college football coaches of all time, Tom Osborne, in his book, <u>Faith In The Game</u>, talks about the implementation of the Unity Council and the positive effect it had on the unity of the teams at Nebraska.

Coach Osborne shares how individuals were chosen from all segments of the football team to come together and form the Unity Council.

Eliminating The Threats

The purpose of the Unity Council was to have weekly meetings in which they reviewed and discussed situations they felt were a threat to team unity; in essence, things that were keeping team members from being able to give 100% each and every play of each practice and each game. Coach Osborne indicated that many times there were minor or things that would seem to some as trivial that came up, yet the members of the Council realized not to treat anything as trivial or take lightly because those very things were enough to cause discontentment and disruption to the unity of the team.

Nebraska had a structure in place where the Unity Council would bring more serious situations to the leadership of the program (coaches) and together they

Eliminating The Threats

would work out solutions and keep the team informed and communicated to. Coach Osborne added that since the Unity Council and coaches were willing to address every concern or complaint, no matter how big or small, it resulted in team members feeling valued and knowing that their thoughts and opinions mattered.

The scope and practice of the Unity Council grew over time. They developed and implemented a point system within their team in which player infractions were given an assessment of points. Once a certain point attainment by a given team member was reached, suspension of that player from the team was an automatic result.

Eliminating The Threats

There was too much risk of distraction and negative impact on the unity of the team to allow the team member to continue as an active part of the team.

It was clear at that point, that the team member was not operating under a self-less approach, was not making sacrifices for the good of the team and was not united under the vision of the team. The team member was bringing to the team all the things that are counter to achieving unity. The Unity Council was allowed to give opinion as to the length of time the suspension was to last as well.

Additionally the Council developed what they called a procedural chart which was a progressional enforcement of consequences (of points) the team

Eliminating The Threats

member's negative actions were accruing. As a result, everyone knew what was expected of each other. There was an expectation that everyone would uphold the team, its members and its unity at all times both on and off the field of play.

They knew any behaviors that were a threat to the team or its unity would not be tolerated and would be swiftly dealt with, with respect, honor and fairness. Thus while administering discipline, the Council and coaches built up team members and still chose to think the best about them.

Earlier it was mentioned a leader has to lead with consistency and fairness.

Eliminating The Threats

Sometimes, in order to protect team unity a leader has to be willing to make a painful decision. It might be suspending a key impact player just before a critical game, but the tough decisions are the ones that will set the standard of expectations for all members of the team as it relates to protecting the unity.

As a leader progresses through the implementation of the things necessary to achieve team unity and guards against the internal and external forces that destroy it, unity will be achieved. The key to protecting that unity and team culture is not compromising on what it took to build and sustain the unity.

Eliminating The Threats

The leader must deal with behaviors and personnel that come against it, while honoring those who are being disciplined, helping them to change their adverse behaviors and becoming a better person in the long run as a result of that change. By both leading and disciplining with a servant's mentality, unity will be established and protected within the team by the leader/coach.

11

Enjoy The Journey… Together!

There is an old proverb that has held true over the years: "All work and no play makes Jack a dull boy." What is the meaning behind that? It means that if a person lives a life of all 'work' they will become dull or bored. They will grow to regret their work and they will not enjoy it.

Enjoy The Journey….Together

Thus they will exude no vibrancy of life or enjoyment thereof. One must enjoy life, and enjoy the team. The team and its members must be able to have that same enjoyment amongst themselves. Understanding, achieving and protecting Team Unity is hard work. Fun must be incorporated into the process. Allow the team and its members to have the opportunity to step away and spend time together as a team, merely enjoying each other's company. The implication of this proverb has proverb or the implication thereto has been used multiple times in films, television shows, novels, songs and shows such as "The Shinning", "The Simpsons", "The Office", "American Dream" (by Casting Crowns), "All Work and No Play" (Husker Du), "My Three Sons", "Twin Peaks", The Batman Series, "Jokers Wild" and more.

Enjoy The Journey….Together

This proverb has been used so frequently over the years because it gives warning to both the leader and the team if they are not allowed to enjoy the journey they are on together.

This is accomplished by allowing the team to take time together and participate in activities outside of 'work' or athletics. Allow them to engage in activities that are focused on others: visiting sick children in a specialty care unit of a hospital or preparing backpacks with school supplies for children and families in need. When team members are involved in activities that are focused on the needs of others and are allowed to see the positive impact of their efforts, they will be better

Enjoy The Journey….Together

equipped in their physical and mental capacities to place the team in higher regard than themselves and will also protect against the things that threaten the team.

Earnest Hemmingway once said, "It is good to have an end to journey toward, but it is the journey that matters in the end." Celebrate the accomplishments together as team no matter how big or small they may be. Remember, when it came to the Unity Council, Coach Tom Osborne remarked that they learned not to allow themselves to view a situation as "trivial" or "minimal" because in so doing, it threatened the unity of the team.

Enjoy The Journey….Together

No accomplishment is too small to celebrate as a team. When parents see the slightest hint of their child taking its first steps, they wildly celebrate the accomplishment by screaming, clapping and cheering loudly. The parents praise their child and encourages them on toward effortlessly walking.

The same should be true for a leader and for a team. An accomplishment or achievement is just that and, no matter how big or small, it is worthy of celebrating. This teaches team members to care about each other and to be able to celebrate the accomplishments (successes) of all teammates thus strengthening team unity.

Enjoy The Journey….Together

This result helps to ensure against the scenario I described earlier of the athlete pushing away his teammates that came up to the end zone to celebrate his touchdown, from existing on a given team. Using the principles outlined in this book will result in a team comprised of members that genuinely care about each other and want success for their fellow team members. A culture of understanding will be developed where, in order to protect team unity, the "whole" must realize the need for a culture that believes and demonstrates, "We are better together."

This culture protects against deep threats to team unity such as pride, gossip, self-focus, comparison and selfishness.

Enjoy The Journey….Together

This type of culture establishes a mindset and realization that being a part of this team is not a job - instead, it is an honor! It has been said, "If you are not fighting for team unity, you are losing team unity." Unity is essential for a healthy team and healthy team members are essential for team unity. Unity takes a lot of effort and intentionality. It is the essence of the sacrifice and commitment discussed earlier in this book.

To protect team unity, the leader and the team members must fight for the team, the team members and the team's goal(s). Enjoy the time with each other. Clemson Football Head Coach, Dabo Swinney is known for the "family-like atmosphere" he creates within his teams.

Enjoy The Journey….Together

Both he and his wife, Kathleen, together have made it a way of life to create a sense of family with the teams they have led over the years. They have modeled carrying for and about others. They have instilled love in the athletes that have played for Coach Swinney.

It is said that Coach Swinney's athletes are not afraid of him, but instead, they see him as family. They know they are safe with him as their coach. They know they are genuinely cared about by Coach Swinney and they are compelled to do what is required, to defy the odds, overcome adversity and obstacles and do what no one else thought possible for them to do or achieve.

Enjoy The Journey….Together

On January 9, 2017, a 13-1 Clemson Tigers Football Team arrived at Raymond James Stadium in Tampa, Florida as an underdog to the 26-0 Alabama Crimson Tide. Alabama was beating opponents by an average of almost 26 points a game and also had one of the top ranked defenses in college football.

Coach Swinney had established an environment of love, trust, care and concern for fellow teammates on that team. He had created an atmosphere where team members were free from fear. They were free from the fear of what others on the team thought of them, free to be who they are.

Enjoy The Journey….Together

They knew they would be honored and accepted and loved as a brother/teammate on that team. When genuine love takes hold of the heart of a team member, that team member will do any and everything necessary to protect the unity that love has created.

There was so much freedom from fear on that team that Coach Swinney freely danced in front of his athletes in post-game celebrations and not once was he ridiculed by them. Team members protected the unity they had by never allowing a media person to speak unfavorably of Coach Swinney's actions nor did they ever speak negatively of him or his actions when interviewed. They knew what Coach Swinney was doing. He was displaying his love for them.

Enjoy The Journey….Together

He strengthened the bond of the unity of team all throughout the season with the eye on the goal. That year the biggest stage in college football came calling presenting the obstacle of the Alabama football juggernaut standing in front of Clemson's "Team Unity" and its goal. The team drew from their unity and overcame and achieved what was said to be an impossible feat - winning the National Championship by beating the University of Alabama.

Even in the face of this great accomplishment, the post-game interviews were filled with players giving credit and recognition to teammates, preferring to celebrate their teammates over the performance and accomplishments of them self.

Enjoy The Journey….Together

It is said that on the day of that big game, Coach Dabo Swinney's message to his team was that, "Winning is about guys [teammates] who play together best, not necessarily are the best players – **and, who care about each other.**"

There is a picture of Coach Dabo Swinney taking the field, positioned in the middle of a line of his players, in which they were all locked arm-in-arm. This picture shows the level of unity they had achieved. It reinforces the impossible can be made possible when unity within a team exists. It is a statement (much like in the game Red Rover, Red Rover) that says, "You send what you want to come against our team, but you will not break it because we are unified!"

Enjoy The Journey….Together

Finally, to the leader and the teammate: Enjoy the journey you and your team are on together. Dare to love. Dare to serve those who are on your team. Seek the best for them and their well-being. Give of yourself to make a teammate's world a little better each day. Sacrifice for the good of the others on your team. Commit to always think the best of those on your team. Commit to giving all you are capable of every day, 100%, for the good of others and the good of the team. Honor everyone. Model what hard work and commitment is and what it means to be a part of a team. Do your assigned job with the character and integrity that empowers and motivates others to do the same.

Enjoy The Journey….Together

Then, then you will understand, achieve and also be able to protect Team Unity. Together, you will accomplish more than you, the team or anyone else thought possible. You'll have an environment, a culture of team unity that others will want to be a part of, will want to join and put their efforts toward. You will have a level of commitment to the unity and success of the team that all who see it know, whatever comes against the team will be turned away and the unity of the team will be defended to the level necessary to overcome and achieve the goal set before it; even if others say it cannot be done.

www.ingramcontent.com/pod-product-compliance
Lightning Source LLC
Chambersburg PA
CBHW030634220526
45463CB00004B/1514